The Longing

Mitchell Ryan Murtoff

Acknowledgement

I would like to thank several people who saw through my dark times when I wrote this poetry. First, I need to thank Chenéy, Jimmy Richards, Joe, Heather, and Maribeth. Along with these friends, I would also like to thank Jen, Cary, Christian, and Ryan. These are friends that spoke with me daily or several times a week once I had to move due to health issues. They are what kept me going. Without such great friends, I probably would not be here today. I would also like to thank my parents Lawrence and Charlotte Murtoff for allowing me to live with them during this time.

The Tiger

A tiger alone in the jungle at night;
Roaming and prowling;
Anticipating the hunt;
A rogue unto his own.

The tiger spots his prey.
Crouching and stalking;
The tiger silently moves in for the kill,
Waiting his destiny to fulfill.

A chase ensued.
An exhilarating chase it became!
Then to his surprise,
A lone tigress gave chase as well.

After the hunt and the chase,
The two become enthralled in a melee,
The tiger crouched and pounced
At the tigress in play.

The two touch noses
And bond together in an immeasurable way.
Now with a litter in tow,
In search of a home by the mythical waterfall they go;
The tiger is no longer a rogue unto his own.

Wild Night Out

I saw a woman entering the club,

Skulking and slinking she came from afar.

Hauntingly irresistible and alluring,

This way she came, her persona strong.

After some dancing,

We said it's ok to be free;

You're just like me.

The sultry dancing became entrancing;

A torrid night it would be

As we both could see.

Then in soft exchanging whispers,

We said let's leave to go someplace afar.

The sun came up

Shining through the window

On a beautiful day.

This was to be the first of many such days;

Because we found each other in a usual way.

That kindred spirit or soul mate;

That met by taking a chance.

The Freak in Me

Complex and eclectic;

Possibly eccentric

Comprise my nature.

Spontaneous yet composed,

Awaiting to meet more people like me;

That are in this way predisposed.

Sometimes a critic or a cynic,

Often times loving and romantic

This is only part of how I feel

Appearing in a dark seductive way.

It's in my eyes,

They don't lie.

It's hard to hide

The freak in me.

Live While I'm Alive

After my world crashed and burned
And I didn't know where to turn,
Along came you.

Live while I'm alive,
Live while I'm alive,
Live while I'm alive.

A breath of fresh air
You helped me through my despair
You helped me to remember to live while I'm alive.

Live while I'm alive,
Live while I'm alive,
Live while I'm alive.

You awakened a part of me
That almost died;
You make me feel alive inside.

Live while I'm alive,
Live while I'm alive,
Live while I'm alive.

Lost in the jungle of doom and gloom,
Your eyes and smile are as bright as the stars
As seen from afar.

Live while I'm alive,
Live while I'm alive,
Live while I'm alive.

Now I am the sun,
And you are the moon;
When we are together a unique beauty shows,
The Aurora Australis around us glows.

Live while I'm alive,
Live while I'm alive,
Live while I'm alive.

AuthorHouse™
1663 Liberty Drive
Bloomington, IN 47403
www.authorhouse.com
Phone: 1 (833) 262-8899

Because of the dynamic nature of the Internet, any web addresses or links contained in this book may have changed since publication and may no longer be valid. The views expressed in this work are solely those of the author and do not necessarily reflect the views of the publisher, and the publisher hereby disclaims any responsibility for them.

Any people depicted in stock imagery provided by Getty Images are models, and such images are being used for illustrative purposes only.
Certain stock imagery © Getty Images.

This book is printed on acid-free paper.

ISBN: 978-1-6655-0388-4 (sc)
ISBN: 978-1-6655-0389-1 (e)

Print information available on the last page.

Published by AuthorHouse 10/08/2020

Printed in the United States
By Bookmasters